CHILDREN OF AIR INDIA

un/authorized exhibits and interjections

a blewointment book

children of air india

UN/AUTHORIZED EXHIBITS AND INTERJECTIONS

Renée Sarojini Saklikar

NIGHTWOOD EDITIONS

2013

Nightwood Editions
P.O. Box 1779
Gibsons, BC V0N 1V0
Canada
www.nightwoodeditions.com

Nightwood Editions acknowledges financial support from the Government of
Canada through the Canada Book Fund and the Canada Council for the Arts, and
from the Province of British Columbia through the British Columbia Arts Council
and the Book Publisher's Tax Credit.

This book has been produced on 100% post-consumer recycled, ancient-forest-free
paper, processed chlorine-free and printed with vegetable-based dyes.

TYPESETTING & COVER DESIGN: Carleton Wilson

Printed and bound in Canada.

LIBRARY AND ARCHIVES CANADA CATALOGUING IN PUBLICATION

Saklikar, Renée Sarojini, 1962-, author
Children of Air India : un/authorized exhibits and interjections
/ Renée Sarojini Saklikar.

ISBN 978-0-88971-287-4 (pbk.)

1. Air-India Flight 182 Bombing Incident, 1985--Poetry. I. Title.

PS8637.A52C45 2013   C811'.6   C2013-903605-9

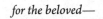

for the beloved—

Contents

Introduction

This is a work of the imagination.
This is a work of fiction, weaving fact in with the fiction,
merging subject-voice with object-voice, the "I" of the author,
submerged, poet-persona : N—
    who loses her aunt and uncle in the bombing of an airplane: Air India Flight 182.

This is a sequence of elegies. This is an essay of fragments:
    a child's battered shoe, a widow's lament—

This is a lament for children, dead, and dead again in representations. Released.
This is a series of transgressions: to name other people's dead, to imagine them.
This is a dirge for the world. This is a tall tale. This is saga, for a nation.
This is about lies. This is about truth.

Another version of this introduction exists.
It has been redacted.

Elegy for Courtroom 20, Vancouver Law Courts

Search gate outside the courtroom.
Citizens security-screened.
Lexan glass to separate
    the body of the court—
public gallery
149 seats and video monitors
    three locations, allowing for unobstructed views.
Everyone watches the proceedings.
A judges' bench accommodates hearings.
23 seats for prosecution and defence counsel,
    in the body of the court.
    Space for 15 lawyers if required.
A witness box, a jury box, both wheelchair accessible.
State-of-the-art technology for use by all courtroom participants.
28 microphones for all participants:
    lawyers, judges, witnesses, translators.
384 service outlets—voice, data, audio, video.
3 forty-inch Plasma Display Monitors.
2 thirty-six-inch TV monitors.
4 voice-activated video cameras transmit proceedings:
    viewing locations outside the courtroom.

    – Government of British Columbia, Court Services, 2003

The room underground: wood panel, red carpet, benches and glass.
The judge a pinprick head,
    far away, behind layers of Lexan
    resinous thermoplastic
    right-angled to the players in the main action—
a drama that was about [redacted] and not about [redacted], family
    reflected, refracted, our airplane saga.

    – N, eyewitness account, March 16, 2005

When confirming your attendance please identify the total number of family members that will attend the ceremony.

PART ONE

in which N imposes meaning

Exhibit: June 23, 1985—detonation
　　　　"in the airplane, a hole blows open,
left aft fuselage, the drop: 31,000 feet, into the Atlantic."

　　　　plan a trip to Ireland—
gather guidebooks: inquiries, reports,
a manifest of passengers, that list always inside:
[name redacted], [name redacted],
[name redacted]—
　　　　　　　　also, [name redacted]
　　　　　　　　who once were aunt and uncle
[redacted], forty-three—
[redacted], forty-five—
　　　　　　　　who once also were husband and wife—
blasted,
　　　　　　fused into links,
　　　　　　　　　　a chain of surnames, [name redacted], [name redacted]

from the archive, the weight—

Everything was normal. Oceans and recovery.
Intense speculation. Partial inflation.

Thirty-nine-point-eight percent. Emotional effects.
Extent and severity. Plastic sheeting.

A chain of command. An orderly fashion.
One hundred-and-thirty-two. Everything was normal.

Passengers and airlines. Lines and comparison.
Volumes and discovery. Cascading failure.

Attached to a limb. Unidentified noise.
Numerous agencies. "Corrections."

Pending and requests. Identified changes.
In lieu of documents. Resource insufficiency.

Protracted and complex. Necessary discussions.
Inadequate security. Eighty-two children under the age of thirteen.

No basis for a claim. And initially cardboard.
Forensic and fallible. A mother and her children.

By sex and by age—a nation and its peoples.
Everything was normal.

A key document. Eye witness,[name redacted].
Employees and agencies. From 2 p.m. each day.

Conclusions based on evidence. No parties with interests.
The status quo. Evidence. A judge. Guilt and innocence.

Ironic. Dissonance. Time and its dimensions—

about N

: in the kitchen, morning, when it first happens—

lacerations,
scald of water
on flesh rising abrasions—
arm, hand, limbs parallel, not seeking a knife, not wanting harm
          harm waits anyway
on the kitchen counter
electric kettle spouts
          steam—

The air

the second time, afternoon,
kitchen, always the site of these discoveries—

          ~~[she was asleep with a slight dent on her nose]~~
          ~~[she was asleep with a slight dent on her nose]~~
          [she was asleep with a slight dent on her nose]

... bloated, peeled apart,
gashes, cuts, deep incisions—
open   body
sing   song of emanations
list the coordinates
mark them
marked bodies
          marks,
these words.

—and her redactions

Q: Where were you born? (colloquial: Where you from?)
N: Poona, India. Pune, India.
Q: Your father? [name redacted]
N: India.
Q: Your mother? [name redacted]
N: India.
Q: But you all, Canadian?
N: Yes-no. Yes/yes.
Q: Your aunt and uncle? Your cousin?
N: India.
Q: Growing up, did you see yourself as part of a community?
N: Newfoundland. Northern Quebec. Montreal.
Q: And then—
N: Small-town Saskatchewan. New Westminster. British.
Q: What's that?
N: British.
Q: What is your purpose in telling this story?
N: Mother, [name redacted]. She—
Q: lost her youngest sister?

Rogue Fragments

What betrayals occur with each telling?
Where is her story? Mother, who was daughter—
She in her saree, who held you in her arms—
She in her saree, big-city girl. Didn't even know how to boil an egg—
Mumbai to St. John's, she in her saree, who married—
What happened?
[Informant to N: "You will need to take out your own story"]

un/authorized invocation

Precursor: British Columbia. It is the early 1980s.

[name redacted], eighteen years old
[name redacted], seventeen years old
[name redacted], sixteen years old
[name redacted], sixteen years old
[name redacted], fifteen years old
[name redacted], Jr., fifteen years old
[name redacted], fourteen years old
[name redacted], thirteen years old
[name redacted], thirteen years old
[name redacted], twelve years old
[name redacted], nine years old

N: speak to me, children of my youth
the years
        inscribe
        suffering to suffering
       what appears, again
           again, the murdered and missing
       singing—
of their song   there will be disinclination. There will be a demand not to—

June 23, 1985. Evening—

fire, here is water: 51°3.6′N 12°49′W

ocean, your name of names

will grow into phytoplankton,

two daughters, inside your topography,

far reaching *Lophelia* interconnect us, *Eunice norvegicus*

today we are made children of the cold water deep—

Sing *Sat Sri Akal*   Sing *Om* and *Shanti*

Fibrous will be the years—

their tentacles tenebrous, how many pieces of flesh?

Count: eighty-two under the age of thirteen.

Before breath, and after, what lies underwater,

one unending song—June 23, 1985.

Memory is a bio-compound.   Add us, and release—

abacus of ritual, underwater and breathing,

we are become echo: God is everywhere. There is no god. There is only history.

There is no history. To our names add each epoch and sing, era Atlantic,

forgetting, released—memory, which is a child. No child, which is a hand. Give us your

hand, this much grief, preposterous. Or, as the poet once said, ridiculous the waste,

sad time. We waltz water with terror, phosphorus longing. The decades to come?

June 23, 1985

joon teyi, oni sao puchaasi

In fragments, add us. In movement, add us.

God is everywhere, nowhere. There is only one time:

nestled cold and coral into its own reef, the after-time.

Give us your wrists to bathe in this chill wind. See the hairs rise.

Minutiae as minute: any living thing.   Until the world ends, end us. Add everything

we did not become. Forget. Remember. Water is nothing but itself.

Where are our names? They are [redacted]. Come Shiva, come Parvati.

Sing, Radha. Add to us: laments from the Upanishads, temple air fanned and brushed—

O Guru Nanak, add the Bible, the Koran, Leviticus and Deuteronomy.

The book of Ruth—alone amid the alien corn. Add us to the wailing wall.
Jerusalem! Jerusalem!   Ocean as container. Come and sing with us.
                Add us, to your memory. Cheek to cheek we dance.
Dance with us, pathos to bathos. Life kisses death.

In water there is fire. Uplifting this tune, heard by no one—

un/authorized interjection

Coroner, [name redacted]:

> "all those expensive lawyers
>> from Toronto & London,
>>> objecting to any mention
>>> of a bomb"

As told to: [name redacted], from email correspondence to N (undated)

Exhibit (1985): nine, four, ten months.

She loves to read,
wins a prize in math.

Her sister follows, arms holding
large heavy books
and behind them,
baby brother.

Status: bodies not found

(list elegy interruption)

Punctured   cracked popped   probed   embedded   bled
                          Eviscerated
         Slashed
                     de   com

Exhibit (1985): fourteen, two months.

When I dance a morning raga
          no injuries to the bone
                    sway or impede
                              my movement

Status: bodies not found

Exhibit (1985): fourteen, eleven.

His brother excels—French, English, math, science—
                    he takes a paper route,
buys milk when an old woman offers two dollars
              with the coins he fetches a carton,
holds it, high—   .

Father: You took her money? She's an old lady.
Son: But Dad, she gave me, she gave—
              I ran all the way.
Father: Take the money back.

He slow-walks
to the woman's house.

*

Before the car drives away, before the plane takes off—
              this paper-route boy
lags behind in his home—
              everyone is waiting—
he touches each piece of furniture,
              goodbye sofa, goodbye lamp—

His arm brushes
against a locked door.

*

Status: It is his brother's body, found.

*

When she hears the news about her paper-route boy, the old woman—
              the woman, old,
when she hears the news—

Exhibit (1985): twelve.

Bombay girl—there is no record of her running—
            the long beaches of Juhu, past high-rise apartments,
                    villas stained bougainvillea red—
        girl bordering into woman,
boundaries not yet formed,
        with her cousins she's in Montreal
they help pack sarees, jewels—
            the night before her first solo journey
                she dreams of waterways, a path leading down
                    to the St. Lawrence,
    in the wash of the river, she'll find two pieces of flat rock.

At the airport, alone past security, she fingers, not pebbles,
                cool metal ridges: her suitcase.

Status: unable to locate body

Exhibit: age unknown.

How he paws at her and she's tiring of him, wants to scold,
        teeth glinting behind a full upper lip,

stop, stop: he's on the verge of crying—howling—

she looks into her child's eyes, and sees past image
to another (the man with whom she made this crying-thing,

don't cry, don't), she sees deeper into the night
this child conceived

a slow seed's insistence—
how can she be so sure. She is. Mother, her child,

whimpering now under her stare,
cornflower blue saree gathering his body—
and over it, a beige sweater, arms around—
        overalls by OshKosh.
These details, this morning, decided.

Status: Mother's body found. Child missing.

File Number: unknown

Notes: This woman, N, believes she is a receptacle—
dead children send her messages.

Observation: She will sometimes mutter, about the other ones. As if
they too clamour to be heard.

*

"[name redacted], St. Isidore de Prescott near Ottawa

[name redacted], over fourteen thousand hours, flight engineer

[name redacted], graduate of Carleton University

[name redacted], co-pilot and war veteran

[name redacted], *a man of the world, 'bon vivant'* from Trois Rivières

[name redacted], nursing student at the University of Guelph…"

un/authorized interjection

Not him! He shouldn't be here. He is here.
Those on the cusp, become centre
                    a gyre
clamours its way—
Air India, always happening, imagine, this bomb-builder boy:
see him running, happy and free, Ludhiana, Chandigarh
(O village of Paldi, O town of Duncan,
all my country-people)
come, stranger, point to this boy
holding his mother's hand on the streets of London
                    stranger, make your pronouncement—
Boy, you will be the one,

[intruder]: if there is childhood—I am on a farm, milking cows—hands on an udder
        and then, and then, and then, and then— in our kitchen, mother makes roti—
It is not June. It is not 1985. No sulphur, no potassium, no cadmium.
Ma, Ma, gurum gram, arreee-bap. Time splits.
I am a young man on Vancouver Island, up river, by the potholes, back-roads dust in
        my face
                    rusted flatbed rattling over rip-rap—

it is only a small fire I make, to cook trout.

in the woods outside Duncan, on the island named Vancouver,
Swedish/Cornish/Punjabi/Chinese/First Nations/Irish/Scottish/Black men work.
Show us the mines, the mills:
sharp, the screeching lathe, sister to a cutting machine
on the green chain, men feed in timber:
cedar, Douglas fir,
the lifeblood of the province
flowing inside a century's worth of work—
mill, mine, marine electrician's shop,
(oh my fellow workers, oh beloved village of Paldi)
on an island, in the woods outside the town of Duncan
boy now man, his turban a sign of holiness,
        stops time

Photo Your Mother, Your Aunt and Uncle, You at the Vancouver Airport 1985

Your Mother wears an Indian outfit/ you and she stand on one side of a glass barrier
a wall/ separation /between/ going staying
Your mother's hand rests on a wooden ledge/dark coloured/
a horizontal line running the length of the photograph
Your Mother a bookend/ one side of the scene
and you/ the other
You wear a blue cotton top/ white cotton pants.
On the other side of the glass/ light/ tarmac behind them your aunt and uncle
in a corridor framed by two sides of glass
Your aunt/separated/glass/barrier/you
Mother, Aunt, Uncle, You
Who frames the photograph/takes the picture/adjusts the camera
Camera Song/Airport Lament/ coming and going
The last view/ Aunt and Uncle/ Who/ Frames?
Where is he/ your father /Unnamed. Absent.
Frozen. Yet/ the credit appears /ever/ with his name
printed in concrete/appears / fronts newspaper/ inside pages/ poster/film/image/still

PART TWO

1985

Exhibit: *is a wire, is a hook*

each decade pulling over and across,
                                        Ireland and the Atlantic,
Canada and its provinces
time catches
            all possible clichés—
let these come and go as they please,
about grieving and grief,
            about time and its dimensions,
about crime and

07:14 dis-
            integrating

overcast intermittent
            the rain

Incident at Mirabel

was assisting
worked for
might contain
no idea
was only
not fully
was moved
on duty
no one at
was airborne
no answer
had already
only to find
left unattended
and requested
was contacted
was overly
able to search
unaccompanied

from the archive, the weight—

there is no reconciliation. There is plausible and implausible.
Catastrophic and unreasonable,

Eighty-two children under the age of thirteen. There is time-consuming and
    inconvenient.
There is manual and reasonably balanced. There are costs.

There is morning: there are the minutes

...   :06
             :07
             :08
             :09
            :10
            :11
            :12
            :13
                        :14
There is Ireland. There is radar.

There is *un-modulated carrier.* There is wave—

frequency and approximately. There are eyes,

and—
here are limbs

and less. There is assignment and number.
There is the register. There is replication of systems. It is incomplete.

Coroner's Office
                City of Cork, County Cork
        .   Ireland

Dear Doctor [name redacted],

You wait for bodies
black bags to the hospital.
Your team assembles:
schedule, arrange, dispense.   ‚
Where is your journal? Pushed aside,
recovered each night, after your shift—
there you are at your desk, elbow and arm pointed
into a pool of lamp light—close my eyes—
vibrations of your being
faint, these undulations:
air, water, memory—
you at your station inside the hospital,
back to a blacked-out window. You are surrounded:
official autopsy reports,

everything accumulates.

                Open the folds of your mind so that
        so that so that so that so that   forward into your life:
a country home, a wife, children and grandchildren.
Where is your journal? Is it true? The fat content of women—
Air India Flight 182,
buoyed their bodies, rising to the surface—Atlantic—
when the men brought them up from the ocean—
what did they see but sockets, empty eyed, these women of the deep,
ocean water pouring through. Sorry to ask these questions,
forgive me, but is it true?

Sincerely,
N

Exhibit No. 1

She boards the plane
                  Indo-Canadian,
this hybrid condition, grown into her bones.

Situation: first solo journey.

Baggage left behind: sister, age eleven.

She is your queen, shimmering fifteen-year-old
you love/hate/love—
the night before Air India Flight 182,
bad dreams propel her—
there you are, together in the bedroom.
                And sweat on your foreheads.

Coroner's Report: "black hair, matted and wound
around a twenty-three-centimetre metal bar
toward the back of the skull."

After the news—
a sister's inventory:
hair, skin, cheekbones—
one ankle, scarred, cross-hatched,
the time she fell off her bike.
It was summer, then, too—
Where are your parents? They will leave you
when they go in search of
her body.

Exhibit No. 2

He runs down a hallway in an airport
                mouth open, at the side of one lip,
                      a curdle of spit.

Brown owl eyes widen his face. Chubby child,
                at the juncture of wrist, ankle—
                      plump smooth skin.

Chattering and loud, he kicks and kicks
                where vinyl seat coverings
join tubular metal, row on row, fists
                open, release
                        find his mother's hair
and he pulls.
            Pull on time, now, child—
            three years old.

Status: unknown

Exhibit No. 3 and eleven months

The meaning of flail:
        body subjected to violent twists and turns—
           a free fall
decompression results,
        all oxygen sucked from blood.

      "damage to the tummy from all that spiralling"

un/authorized interjection: embalmer, [name redacted]

Exhibit No. 4

She studies hard
        Etobicoke girl, suburban with duty
        be good
        be the best
        do more
        marry well
        duty is everything—family,
        everything. She excels: track and field, grass hockey
           biology, history—
               girls flock to her, a few boys,
                   also. The trip to India, reward
        for being good.
The night before Air India Flight 182,
        she sneaks away from the officially sanctioned party
           to the dugout by the school, drinks cherry brandy, eats
           oatmeal cookies,
(her parents would *kill* her if they knew).
On the way home, nausea rises but she damps it down. Good girl—
doesn't look her mother in the eye
        late, late, where have you been?
(oatmeal curdling, cherry brandy burbling)
mother's voice a needle—stitched to daughter,
button eyes
dart back
and forth to the bedroom where father snores—
sounds to fill a house.
In the foyer, a line of packed suitcases, bulging with gifts,
bulging with a mother's invective:
Deekrah, are you crazy,
what kind of girl, have you no pride,
such shame, why didn't you call us, where are your things
don't you know how early—bad daughter.
The hiss of her mother's voice
follows upstairs, in the bathroom,

click the lock
shut out the mother still outside stage whispering dry disapproval
finally, the toilet lid opens, seat raises
mouth to bowl, and she releases
her oatmeal cherry mixture
bright pink
not deep enough for red.

Status: unknown.

Exhibit No. 5

He burrows deeper
      twin bed comforter emblazoned with cartoon figures
      soon to be flung off
      Mississauga to India
      set for a journey—summer vacation—he is thirteen, just waking, a pulse
      flows groin to feet—toes, ankles, calf muscles
      hand on himself—hair curled around balls, cock
      thinking of girls, wetness too viscous to be perspiration—
hips, thighs, chest, throat,
      Adam's apple: prominent,
boy, almost man, soon to be ended
even though his morning actions
      grasp life.
Only one groan escapes, sound too small for warning—
      what if we were able to stand at the foot of this boy's bed,
      our smiles lopsided, cheeks stained red, flushing
still able to say: boy, take your body-pleasure,
this first, this last time.
On the plane, centre aisle, in the crook of his arm,
a school text hides
Marvel comics: Superman, Spider-Man
fly off magazines—
at the time of detonation.

Status: Body recovered. See Coroner's Report for details.

Exhibit No. 6

She plays ice hockey
        fast—the scrape of ice on the edge of her blade—
Grade eight graduation:
        the night before Flight 182. She's soft-
spoken,
held within this enclosure: friends from school
        and her brother's laugh.

Status: body not found.

interjection non/autorisée

l'équipe du coroner/légiste (notes): [expurgé], [expurgé], [expurgé] et [expurgé].

Démembré(e)

BLESSURES EXTERNES

[elle était endormie avec une légère entaille/bosse sur le nez]

[elle était endormie avec une légère entaille sur le nez]

[elle était endormie avec une légère entaille sur le nez]

une couleur plus intense

l'océan (re)tient

[expurgé], [expurgé], [expurgé], et [expurgé]

un/authorized interjection: Coroner's team (notes): [name redacted], [name redacted], [name redacted] and [name redacted].

dismembered

EXTERNAL INJURIES

[she was asleep with a slight dent on her nose]

a deeper colour

the ocean holds

EXTERNAL INJURIES

Abrasions Reviewed: nose penetrated

Maxillary antrum

Femur, forearm, heel

Abdomen wound (ed).

Exhibit: 1985—stitch, stitch, stitch

and in the book
there are the names
look up the name of the child
to be seated in the last row of the plane
he is jumping up and down in the aisle, his mother cannot restrain him.
Soon, soon, he will visit the cockpit—

Query: what was the velocity of the plane when it hit the Atlantic?

Coroner's report: sometimes the decompression flattened bones

Testimony: all they found were dozens of dead sharks

intertidal memory: six thousand feet below the ocean's surface

Exhibit: June 23, 1985, about the body—

body's attire:
blue-grey slacks
                white belt
                Givenchy tie
                black socks,
fine gauge wool
                one Daks shoe,
                        hand-waxed
        one wallet,
goatskin

body's list:
                left leg
                left foot
                left shoulder
                left thigh

body's verbs:
                distended
                extended
                bent
                wrenched

body's objects:
                pick
                chunk
                metal

body's song:
                twist me
                I break all water
                        washes

PART THREE

in the after-time

Exhibit N: *This page, laboratory—1985, bending, bent,*

on a tarmac by the ocean an airplane waits,
blunt nosed, round bellied—who will sit in it
          walk in it, eat in it, shit in it
hands on passports,
clench   release
shoes slip off at security
limbs surrender to scrutiny
X-rayed and scanned
          flying across Canada to Ireland
(row sixteen, seats b and c, midway by the door)
          province after province, name after name,
fingers link
then open   link   then open
hands anticipate anemones
          flowers of the Atlantic. No magic exists,
that flowers may rise and fly over rock, prairie, water—
          the sky is not an impartial judge—the sky plays favourites:
          jagged, not sheet lightning, cumulus over cirrus
flying-remembering-forgetting
grammar fuselage or oil
               songs or engine
bodies or wings
                 time

from the archive, a continuance

Into this saga, there is always one continuous intervener:
June 23, 1985. There are experts and departments.

There are multiple actors. There are steps taken, untaken.
There are phenomena and failure. There is extremism.

There is Ottawa and Vancouver, Montreal and Duncan,
Norita and County Cork. There is regularly informing.

There are telexes, seen and unseen. There are policies.
There are protocols and additional measures.

There is heightened and weekends. There are the dogs.
There is the waiting. There is confusion.

There are frontline workers. There is optimal security.
There is threat fatigue. There is secrecy.

There is the conflation of several events. There is memory.
There is assessment. There is circulation.

There are eighty-two children under the age of thirteen.
There are dossiers, chronologies, rules, conclusions.

There is the basis of evidence. There is plausibility and credit.
There is interception. There is threat. There is the highest regard.

There are flotsam and jetsam. There are no records of reports.
There are reports. There are agencies and roadblocks.

Regimes and tribunals. Deficiencies and incidents.
Illustrations and charts.

Claims and contradictions.
Special procedural challenges.

There are eighty-two children—

un/authorized invocation

women of Prince George,
women of Vancouver,
women of Ciudad Juarez,
your long reach, a continent's bones—
        Anchorage to Prince Rupert,
        Vancouver to San Diego, and then inland—
Speak, women to N
absolve any heresy—
        is it, is it, is it, is it, is it
        wrong to—?
In the after-time the future accumulates forward and back—
        June 23, 1985.
This is British Columbia,
and of you, women of North America,
there is the not recorded, the not allowed:
your ecosphere where currents rise—
navigate to feel them, walk any road to sense—
It is June, 1985: unknowable presence that speaks—
Come, who murders,
who remains, in this life, in the next
in history, in the text made to be material,
and believe, and refuse to believe, the living, the dead
where is
        totality murdered, missing
        air   an entire coastline, stratosphere of suffering,
        with such force future
becomes past,
manifest in biosphere
dome to cover atrocities one to another—
this proposition arises from rock, from the shelf of mountains:
all murdered souls congregate
and speak. Speak, missing and murdered women
to N, to the children of Air India, atrocity to atrocity
a common language

opening passages in time
and its dimensions, where messages may travel—

C-A-N-A-D-A: in the after-time, always, there is also the before—

June 23, 1985
punctured, probed
embedded
sediments—
other peoples' stories
cracks within cracks,
tales, anecdotes
gossip, family legends
tied knots   twist
in N's left gut, nation, in her, a body of provinces
when she walks down to the river
each story-bit
a laceration
inside her deep down
secrets
dismembered
one limb after another—
incident as saga, saga as tragedy,
tragedy as occurrence
so what a plane explodes
so what people die, they die every day
in her body, blast and counter blast
(Air India Flight 182)
her story and the stories of other people
interact—a toxin?
Alloy, mixed suffering:
name the Ukraine, find the Doukhobors, ferret out head taxes,
also, Cambodia, Ireland,
the bombing of Britain,
Guernica, Dresden,
Gaza, Afghanistan,
Khymer, Ararat, all such entries in any such list, incomplete,
Auschwitz (shush, shush)
each name

releases vibrations
Komagata Maru
internment and confiscation
words tremble
into this cornered saga, a litter
suppressing action,
an accumulation—

                    and there is N, down at the river—

lumber on the docks, metals underground
salmon on the pier,
how the dates, such flies, buzz
1888–1910–1945–1947–1967–1985
also, add 1907, 1911, 1914, 1962, 1997
and after,
scandal and song
rise up, Air India, portal,
the river, a conduit,
each comer's story
a stain on a shack, lean-to, split-level house, hall, lodge,
grocery mart, train station, bridge, railroad,
condo tower, SkyTrain tracks
emanating messages—hoarded in hoax nation,
a-taking-and-a-taking, this country
receiver of peoples, and always underneath, the everlasting story—
this is how we suffered
list each band, tribe, linguistic group, hereditary chief
no accounting with those names, not released to her
because not student enough, not seeker enough
not listener enough, each tale incoming
woven unending saga,
citizens,
settlers,
first nations,
neighbours,
families, loners,
saints, thieves,

liars and fine upstanding sons
daughters as receptacles
holding, holding
C-A-N-A-D-A,
once she sang—

Exhibit: where visitations occur

The kick of my leg. The kick of my leg. The edge of my blade. The edge of my blade.
Soccer and hockey. I was that kind of Canadian boy—
             ask Father about practice, drive with him to the arena
                   sit with him
                   inside, air cold enough to lock down memory,
                         movement is hinge:
             ask Father to walk
                   with you to the edge—
                   park where I played.
In movement, release.
In movement, release.
                         Father will tell you how smart
                         I am math–sciences–French–English—
                                           Language scrapes
                   against my edge
       Indian-Canadian-English-French
             melt   icicle dialects
                         These fragments butt, skull to grass—
follow Father home
Is my room still as it was? The year of my death. The year of my death,
             kick down the doors and scrape,
                                           edge of a basement floor.
List every item in my bedroom. Look for hockey posters.
             Bodies gyrate. Rock stars jump, knees bend
                   laminated cardboard : insert names here. They are redacted.
                   Ask Father to play Sony for you.
                   There is my Walkman   my electronic inventions.
Ask Father to stop roaming the rooms of our home.
If you cannot find him, he will have joined me. Ask us about joining,
             about water, ice, grass.
                   These words are fields.
open   close
       kick
                   scrape memory

run to the wall.
Open   yourself to seeing
                    there are the children, there—

Status: body recovered?

Exhibit: the censor that is Time inserts this sutra,

also raga and un/authorized

a tabla!   Strings of a sitar   body encodes fable
June 23, 1985: *joon teyi, oni sao puchaasi*   insistence
If she were breath—
fire
If she were mineral—
copper
If she were jewel—
ruby
Once,
upon time, this dancing girl ends in water—
Where? In soul's mother, the ocean—
once
upon time
this girl dances
June 23, 1985   taking and taken,
this girl, [name redacted], from this family [name redacted]

Officers of the Court!   Record a lineage
old as iron, *sean le hiarann*

—on the plains of the Punjab, in the footsteps of the Himalayas,
a burrowing wind—there is no locale   there is just the after-time
always and [name redacted]
who is soul and dancing-girl,
bifurcated
and become sister
and their breath *saah ohna de*
and their breath,   *agus a nanáil*
now Chinook
Ah, spring   in winter   if there is a city, it is
[name redacted]

O Officialdom!   List the names, the girls dance—
            find them in the time that is always
June 23, 1985
This is a morning song for all the children of Air India Flight 182,
            airplane of the Emperor, *Kanishka*.

Elegy: what it feels like after

I

n: What will always be missing?
N: Sing. Do not sing(h).

n: She lies in a darkened bedroom, head wrapped in a blue sweater.
N: Sing of the days just after the bomb. Do not sing.

n: She is the mother who does not speak. Speak, who does not touch. Touch.
N: Was there no daughter to comfort her?

n: Shunned, also.
N: So many details to withhold. Tell them. Do tell them.

n: Do not listen to this daughter. With a finger she will stroke the skin of the mother.
N: Rigid memories produce ill-fitting songs. This is no song.

n: And of dreams, before the bombing?
N: Find she who is mother who was sister. What kind of daughter refuses all songs?

n: Why not consult the record that is the saga of the bombing of the plane?
N: It is all there. There is nothing.

II

N speaks to a reporter. Story. Saga.
Testimony. Lies. Cellphone.
Judge. Children. Dismiss.
N speaks to a reporter.
I used to believe, the reporter says.
N speaks.
I used to believe, the reporter says, that one day,
there'd be more criminal charges.
I used to believe, the reporter says,
            but now I see. After this inquiry, that'll be the end. Sorry. That'll be the end.
N speaks to a reporter. You going to Ireland, this year?
You going to Ireland, this year? You going to Ireland this year?
N speaks to a reporter. Story. Sorry. Saga.
What's it like to be part of the Air India story?
N speaks to a reporter.

III

In the home-house, in the basement, there is the mother— she is singing a sweet song.
It is before—
June   1985

        Of her name, there are redactions.
        Of her mother tongue, there is no record—
                this is the life of a woman, made in India,
                    living in Canada.

In the home-house, in the basement, there is the mother
       And she is absent, sister

C-A-N-A-D-A: in the after-time, always there is also the before—

-June 23, 1985 threads filaments-land-water-air spirits-list every nation-

██████████████████

-immigrant-imminent-
    -arrival-   -dispossession- -carry-over-   -a-chain-of-tales-
-Air India-disruption?
    -the way of things: ███████████████
    what is not mentioned?   These markers:

before,

is a place.   History as surveillance,
    comes a morning and a plane: Boeing-747-*Kaniskha-become-Montreal*
    -Air India Flight-181-become departure-become-Air India Flight 182

      and sweep, *Ballygreen, Ballygreen,*
      air space transponder

        ██████ and vanishing

    the air   before and after
      [marker to be excised: ~~September 11, 2001~~]

inside
outside, the names—although we may live,

fortified with the present, our encampment
      at the dinner table, at the mall, in the boardroom, on the
      street
          there we are, standing in line
electronic gadget   *Ballygreen, Ballygreen,* echolocation and find us—

hold close, tear apart
    handshake. Head/nod. Head Tax. Eyes downcast. Look away.
    Look right at—

stitch-before-to-after-
          -before-1985-to-after:
      time inflamed
dis-and-integrate   ~~we never speak of it~~

Informant to N: in the after-time

My name is [redacted] and my mother was [redacted].
I was three months old when my mother died.
I am without memory of my mother. I am not familiar with this record of events.
June 23, 1985 and after.
I get older. I am her only child.

Narita: *hymnal-acro-nym*

[name redacted] [name redacted]

ACI ACISS ACPA ACS ADO ADR AG AGAS AGBC AGC AI AICCA
AICVWS AITF AIVFA AKJ ALAA ALPA AML AML/ATF AML/CFT
ACI ACISS ACPA ACS ADO ADR AG AGAS AGBC AGC AI AICCA
AICVWS AITF AIVFA AKJ ALAA ALPA AML AML/ATF AML/CFT
APEC API/PNR// APO ARAACP ASIO ATA aTAC ATF ATFT ATSC AVSEC BC BK BOAC BPR BSO
BSS C// CAC CACPCACPP CAFAS CAIR-CAN CA   CATSA CBA CBCR CI CISA
CISR C-CAT CCD CCLA CCSI CCTV C Directorate,   CIB CIC CIFFA CIO CIP CIS
CISBC CI&W CJC CLA AICVWS AITF AIVFA AKJ A   L/ATF AML/CFTAPEC API/
PNR// APO ARAACP ASIO ATA aTAC ATF ATFT A   OAC BPR BSO BSS C// CAC
CACPCACPP CAFAS CAIRX CTC//CTF DSSO DTF   EDS EDT EDU E&FE// EFTR
EVD FAA FATF FAU FBO FININT FINTRAC // FIU FLQ FLSC FMCMV/IN // GA GOC GOI GTTA
HBS HHMD HQ IAB IAC IATA IBET I/C ICAO ICLT ICSI // IED IG IMF IM/IM INSET Insp.or Inspt.
IO IPOC IR IRPA I&S ISO ISYF IT ITA ITAC IVTS JFO JIC JMT LC LCTR LO LITE MANPAD MATRA
MI5 MILF ML MLAT // MOA MOT MOU RAIC RAP RAW // RAIC RAP RAW // RCMP RCMP SS RFID
RIUNSTR // SAC SDS SeMS Sgt. SIGINT SIRC SIT SLO SOP SOS SPL SPOT SPP SPROS SQ SR SRAS
SS SSCMS SSEA S/Sgt SSO STR STS TA TAP   TFU TIPS NTX TPR TSA TSC TWA
U/F UK U/M UNAQTR UN CTC // UNSTR   VIA VIIU VIP VIR VPD VSI WAC&R
WPP WPPA WRC WSO WTM WTMD XRT   C IR IRPA I&S ISO ISF IT ITA ITAC
IVTS JFO JIC JMT LC LCTR LO LITE MAN   ILF ML MLAT // MOA MOT MOU
MSB NAPSP NC NCCT NCIB NCIS // NCO   RC SIT SLO SOP SOS SPL SPOT SPP
SPROS SQ SR SRAS SS SSCMS SSEA S/Sgt SSO STR STS TA TAPP TARC TAU TC TF TFU TIPS NTX
TPR TSA TSC TWA U/F UK U/M UNAQTR UN WTMD XRT
APEC API/PNR// APO ARAACP ASIO ATA aTAC ATF ATFT ATSC AVSEC BC BK BOAC BPR BSO
BSS C// CI&W CJC CLA CLEU CMCLA CO CO CP or CP Air CP CPC CPIC CRA CRCVC CRSIA CS
CSC CSE CSEC CSIS C/Supt. CT CT or CAT, CT-X CTC//CTF DDG, ops DDR DEA DFAIT DG DHA
DIO DND DNI DOJ DOT DPP DSSO DTP EACSR ECAC EDD EDS EDT EDU E&FE// EFTR EVD FAA
FATF FAU FBO FININT FINTRAC // FIU FLQ FLSC FMCMV/IN // GA GOC GOI GTTA HBS HHMD
HQ IAB IAC IATA IBET I/C ICAO ICLT ICSI // IED IG IMF IM/IM INSET
Insp.or Inspt. IO IPOC IR IRPA I&S ISO ISYF IT ITA ITAC IVTS JFO JIC JMT LC LCTR LO LITE MAN-
PAD MATRA MI5 MILF ML MLAT // MOA MOT MOU MSB NAPSP NC NCCT NCIB NCIS // NCO
NPO NPRM NPS NSA NSCNSCIS NSE NSID NSIS NSOB NSOS NSOTF NSR NSTAS NSY SB OAS OAS
OCP IOC OP OPC OPP ops OSA OSCE OSFI // PBS PC PCMLTFA // PCO P Directorate PEP PFLP
PHRO PIA // PIRS PMO POC PPP PRPF PS or PSC PSD PSEPC PSU PTV QPF RAD // RAIC RAP RAW
// RAIC RAP RAW // RCMP RCMP SS RFID RIUNSTR // SAC SDS SeMS Sgt. SIGINT SIRC SIT SLO
SOP SOS SPL SPOT SPP SPROS SQ SR SRAS SS SSCMS SSEA S/Sgt SSO STR STS TA TAPP TARC TAU
TC TF TFU TIPS NTX TPR TSA TSC TWA U/F UK U/M UNAQTR UN CTC // UNSTR US USAP
USSS VDS VIA VIIU VIP VIR VPD VSI WAC&R WPP WPPA WRC WSO WTM WTMD XRT

Voir Dire

June, 1985—

a singing tale,

the future, unheard

if you are N, you are twenty-three and you are willing to confess

to curiosities about death, about who is mourned, who is effaced,

but your confession is of little interest.

It is June 1985 and you will resist the impulse to conflate stories of suffering.

You will sit on your hands, if you have to think:

about murderers,

about families,

your hands know very little

about the layers that will greet you

in the time that will come after and in the after-time

there will be the place that is British

and Columbia and its land and time

will layer in ways that will be unreadable—

You will sit upstairs in the home-house,

820 Dublin street where once as a girl, you screamed

at your parents, *I hate you, I hate you*

and of hate, and its layers in a province

you will have only this limited understanding.

*

It is June, 1985. Upstairs in the home-house

you conduct name experiments:

>you will try on British surnames instead of your own;

>you will not try to say the name of your dead aunt;

>you will have no knowledge, no memory, no premonition, no

>visitation of such a name ~~as the name of a woman~~,

>who will be murdered or missing and such things will be

>unknown;

you will practise writing your signature; you will write out the names of the women

you meet: Anne, Julie, Rebecca, Cindy, Christine, Valerie, Patty, Jane, Mary, Grace,

Gloria, Violette, Emily, Olympe, Michelle, Kathleen, Bernadine, Lisa. And these

names will mean nothing to you. There will be nothing for you in that cadence that

is the falling of their names. There you are, upstairs, in the home-house, 820 Dublin

Street, New Westminster, British Columbia. The cosseting that is *pax Canadiana*—

country as collective, wide deep box where all rough things smooth over,

stories in compartments, separate and apart, safe,

>will by year's end, mean nothing to you.

It is June, 1985. You are N—

>What will you decide, in the case that is the saga called Air India?

>Well, you have your tricks,

>>and your ways.

June 23, 1985

[a wolf jaw opens and we fall in]

that day early

    there is the morning telephone, it is raucous

ringing! ringing!

    there is the mother

screaming seconds minutes

    elongated hours

    the day—

into late morning

        the news of the bombing of an airplane

into the community that is all the people of the life that is the life—

     they visit, up at the manse, the old home-house in its place, 820 Dublin

     Street. Yes. They bring food. And tears. These Canadians,

they sit on the faux–French provincial sofa, purchased at Woodward's, uptown New

West. Everyone talks about how fine the summer has been, how great the weather,

how much everyone enjoyed meeting Aunty and Uncle—*She was so happy, radiant,*

what a nice couple, how terrible. They were so relaxed. Yes. On vacation but they miss

their only son.

They will go home earlier,

     to be with—

afternoon,

    everyone cries—

        the image of the dead, fresh.

What? There is no image.

What? There are images produced.

There is the state broadcaster: *maa-baap*. Mother–Father.

    un/authorized interjection:

    Missionary to subaltern: There is the crown, India is the jewel. There is the

    queen. She is the empire. *Taro maa-baap.*

Subaltern: response, removed.

There is the image. What? Over and over, scenes of water, choppy and grey—

    fuselage

        broken wing of a plane

Men in boats on the waters off the Irish Coast, these images,

in the piano room away from the stream of people who visit the home-house on

Dublin Street, on they come, each one with some offering: baked chicken, white

rolls, potato salad, in the piano room, there are no images. There are images. There

are no images. There are images. There is the country, Ireland. There is the country,

India. There is the country, Canada. There is the province: Columbia, that is British

that is no country but layers in early evening. June 23, 1985. About a plane that

disappears somewhere over the Atlantic. And it is about Aunty and Uncle. No one

says the name of the young son,

        left behind.

Another version of this moment exists.

Dispatched, there is fetching, there is the other cousin. He must be brought,

Vancouver to New Westminster.

There is the boyfriend. He drives downtown from suburb to city. He drives a red

cougar, muscular two-door car, white bucket seats,

to Vancouver from New Westminster, down to the city and back again, the ride

home.

Not much noise on a Sunday in Vancouver in 1985.

Hide in the piano room in the house at 820 Dublin Street. Watch TV.

There are no images. There are the images.

Excise from this record all other mentions of the car, its owner, the year, the not

wanting

to drive, the morning resistant to any mention of—

Another version of this moment exists.

(Interjection: Informant: "As soon as he got her call, I don't know how she knew he

was in town, and where were her own folks, I wonder, well anyways, he just took off,

told me not to bother him, he just run out to his car and out of the house.")

Another version of this moment exists.

The sun slants across the linoleum floor of the kitchen in the home-house.

Stand in the kitchen with a man, elder in the church where family belongs. It is a belonging-church. Stand with the man who comes from Mennonite stock, from a hamlet in southern Saskatchewan. He met his wife there. The man is tall with a low, bass voice. His eyes take in everything, magnified by glasses, every person he meets is brought in under his gaze. His wife is pale-skinned, blue-eyed, her flesh like loaves of freshly baked bread. There is standing.

It is the kitchen.

It is the home-house at 820 Dublin street.

Another version of this moment exists.

In the kitchen at the home-house by the white fridge whose contours curve and dip,

1940s prairie kitchen fridge, Frigidaire, a castoff for the manse.

The woman with blue eyes and a halo of white hair: she is bending.

Look, there are the tears. There is her story which is her brother, named—

He is twenty years old. He will join the Big War and he will be soldier, he will be:

Pvt. [name redacted], L[numbers redacted], Calgary Highlanders, RCIC

and is dying. Another version

of his moment exists   there is the woman, blue eyes in

the home-house in the time that is June 23, 1985 and she is speaking:

"I still miss him. Think of that."

Another version of this moment is standing beside the woman who misses her brother

June 23   1985   evening light by the white fridge   by the woman with blue eyes

by the brother who is dying by N in the home-house, 820 Dublin Street.

Time before and after and always, the name ~~of the young boy left behind~~ not

mentioned. Cousin.

Another version of this moment exists. It is excised from this diary.

Do not mention any names. Insert all relevant names. They are redacted.

June 23, 1985. Evening. At the home-house. 820 Dublin Street.

New Westminster, British Columbia.

N: at the home-house, forever and

opening

a box of documents, a trunk full of sarees.

Where are the stories? They are here and not here.

N is in the home-house, on Dublin Street in the town of the towns,

      in the past that is always—

      :

There is Aunty [name redacted], side by side with N

on a sofa in the living room.

Sideways there is looking. There in the groove of Aunty's nose, a star-shaped

diamond flickers. And there are bangles to rub against wrists against N's arm.

      Aunty laughs.

Aunty: We'll go home earlier because—

N: Why? Stay.

Aunty: We'll go home earlier because I miss him. He's only a young boy.

N: You must miss him.

Uncle: We will re-book our flights.

Aunty: Yes. We'll go home earlier because—

N: no, no, stay,

N's mother: stay, stay.

Aunty and Uncle: Our son.

      All: June, 1985.

      *

There they are. Aunt and niece on a sofa, faux–French provincial, purchased

in the store of stores, Woodward's, atop the hill in the town of towns.

There is N, a young woman, mother of no one.

Observation:

when Aunty laughs, her teeth, bold and white

interjection

"... a twelve-year-old boy, darling of the house, so pampered... suddenly turned into an orphan with very few good and honest relatives ... very hard for me ... to explain all these years ... grew up learning how mean this world ... none of the governments of ... ever cared to ask..."

Witness No. [redacted]—Name [redacted]

Air India Inquiry

from the after-time, N's excisions

Dear ~~Irfan~~, will you ever visit Ahakista, County Cork, Ireland?

Dear ~~Irfan~~, does religion bring you comfort?

Dear ~~Irfan~~, pardon me for mentioning, I do think of them, your parents

Dear ~~Irfan~~, your mother the gardai found, your father, lost—

Dear ~~Irfan~~, pardon me for mentioning, I—

Dear ~~Irfan~~, to say Ireland/India, is to hear old songs

Dear ~~Irfan~~, there will be records. Stored and kept.

Dear ~~Irfan~~, there will be, time, at Cork, the waves

Dear ~~Irfan~~, one day I will rise and go and come to Ahakista

Dear ~~Irfan~~, on the Inner Net, it says to say, *Atha Ciste*

Dear ~~Irfan~~, halfway along the Sheep's Head, between Durrus and Kilcrohane

Dear ~~Irfan~~, I imagine that coast and—

Dear ~~Irfan~~, how the years count themselves up…

Dear ~~Irfan~~, time is an un/wanted snoop

Dear ~~Irfan~~, I see on the Inner Net, how you are bodybuilding

Dear ~~Irfan~~, now we are *friends* and I see—

Dear ~~Irfan~~, my fingers click a device over your words, *like*

Dear ~~Irfan~~, I never see photographs of your wife and—

Dear ~~Irfan~~, last night I watched another machine.

    black and white movie
    Hitchcock. The 1940s:
        people flung from an aircraft out onto debris
        wing of a plane   into make-believe Atlantic
        manufactured wind,   rain thatoldmoviemagic

All the actors survive.

CHAPTER II: THE INQUIRY PROCESS

MR. ████████ [...] There's been some reference in our hearings to a culture of secrecy that pervades Ottawa. Do you have any comment on that characterization?

MR. ████████ I think it's an accurate characterization.

MR. ████████ Accurate or inaccurate?

MR. ████████ Accurate. It's accurate. We over classify, we over-redact and then we ultimately get embarrassed by it being shown to not have been necessary so many times. I think it's just in the nature of the beast, and that happens all the time, and it happens continuously before every inquiry that seems to take place. We start from the position of we're not going to share, we're not going to show anything because we don't want to reveal anything and then, ultimately, we have to reveal, and we have to show, and the system gets embarrassed because of some obvious, you know, classifications that were clearly inappropriate and so on.

PART FOUR

in the woods, outside Duncan, British Columbia

Exhibit: *Coroner's report, city of Cork, autopsy file*
　　　　"We picked them up at sea, nearly all women—

　　　　　floating."

Edge of Ireland, transcript
　　　　outcropping of rock, proceeding,
　　　　　　　names as luggage—[redacted], [redacted], [redacted]—add to
　　　　　　　a village
Ahakista: one church, two pubs,
　　　　inhabitant: Atlantic,
　　　　memory orphans June 23, 1985
　　　　a widow,
　　　　　　　who lists the names of eighty-two children under the age of thirteen
　　　　faces in a sundial the hours and a garden, a wall,
　　　　　　three hundred and twenty-nine, thirty, thirty-one
　　　　　　deposited in stone, the flesh of names,
　　　flower and rot　　　　remember-forget
　　　time and its dimensions
transmute breath and breathe
inside the chamber rooms of the Atlantic, search unerring
　　　　this ability: locate a site of contact
airplane to ocean's surface
　　　　then down,
through the years not erased　　　uncovered
　　　　　kick up underwater debris
　　　　　　time enlarges
　　　　doors, rotted seat frames,
　　　　　　　rusted spans of once-shiny material, this wreckage.
　　　　　　　　Does N find an uncle? She does not.
　　　　　　　　　Aunt's body, released years ago

from the archive, the weight

Air India/Canada. Canada/Air India.
Into this saga, there is 1985 and after in the after-time,

there is no doubt. There is judgment. Do not recall.
Appropriate limitations. Temples-gurdwaras-churches-synagogues.

Truth and its exemplar. [Emphasis added]
Limited time, limited pain. Vital interests.

Exhibits and suspicion. The public interest.
Federal and provincial. Over-classification. Over-

redaction. Rules of Practice. Happens all the time.
A judge. The accused. Credibility and children: under age,

under ocean. Inappropriate classifications. Tapes and wiretaps.
Malice and intention. Identification of relevant information.

Endless hours. A judge. Eighty-two children.
Specific references. Assumptions.

Endless hours. It can only be hoped.
Monuments and memorials.

Requests and charges. Staff and agencies. Frequency and coordinates.
Formulations and charges. Compilations and purposes.

Current procedures. Tens of thousands. Indices.
Redactions. Songs. Prayers. Effective notice.

Yielding and data. Mountains and ocean.
Thorough and slow. Terms of Reference.

Fulfillment and impartiality. Stonewalling. Sections.
Charter and contributions. Open. Close. Transparent,

time—

Paldi/Duncan

         in high school, in British Columbia, in the 1980s,
no one teaches the name of this village,
         Paldi,
         name latitude 48° 47' 00"
         name longitude 123° 51' 00"

         exists / does not exist—
         list the distances,
Paldi to Duncan, sing(h)
Gazetteer, on your map (92B/13)
         north side, Cowichan River, west of Duncan, Sahtlam Land District
how close they nestle, these two, a village, a town, together
apart, the distance, India to Canada:
Empire is woven, it is one continuous journey, Sing(h)!
Duncan to Ahakista
Canada to Ireland
June 23, 1985—where is the after-time?

Exhibit: in the woods, outside Duncan, British Columbia

That a bomb is made. That is known.
That the bomb is set off, that is known, in the woods, outside Duncan, cousin-
town
        to the village Paldi.

*

Of all the locations in Empire, real and imagined, past and present,
        It is here: June 1985,
there are no straight lines—

if there is a man, he is making detonation—

      Time loads up incident.
      In recounting there is implication.
      Describe all particulars.

      Piney scented,
         the woods.   Where *is*
the past
          also present

we never speak of it

It is June, 1985.

Piney scented, the names layer precedent
the years before, counted in arrivals,
claims, transfers of title, appropriations, settler-developments—
   There are the names. They are redacted,
nevertheless conveyed. Empire's instruments:
    deed, act, gazette and catalogue.

There is the province. It is British and layered. It is others, as well.
There is the founding. There are the names. Duncan. Paldi.
   And the woods.
There is the temple, before—

Exhibit: 1906, subaltern sutra

Speak
              about the tatters of history, thrown road-side,
there is a signal : 1906, comes a man, [name redacted],
he is India to Canada   he is the lore that is the founding.
Let the name stand.

Paldi

[*un/authorized interjection:* at the Legislative Library, Victoria,
            British/Columbia: Librarian: "there's not much here, about Paldi."   ]

              Rag-bit story-village,
                    empire's jewel-India
                         colony's outpost: sing, Cowichan,

~~Quamichan/Kw'amutsun Clemclemaluts (L'uml'umuluts), Comiaken (Qwum'~~
~~yiqun'), Khenipsen (Hinupsum), Kilpahlas (Tl'ulpalus), Koksilah (Hwul-~~
~~qwselu), and Somena (S'amuna')~~

                         of your valley,
                                   ask those in Duncan, sister/cousin town:

What happened in the woods? Ask, ask, what happened in the woods?
Show us the way to Paldi—

we never speak of it

Raga for Dominion Day: a *Jor Mela* in Paldi, British Columbia

Translation required: Punjabi into Hindi, into Cowichan, into Japanese and Cantonese, about the founding of the village of Paldi and about the man,

Shri-श्री [name redacted], British Subject
>   who intersects time, 1906
into a century, a man and his brothers
authorized entry—
>   Action: there are the trees sold into logs
>   Action: there is the business of timber to lumber, sold by the board
>   Action: there are three men, Japanese and invited
there is a sawmill, *saw you*
whom my soul loves,
>   lumber stacker, the man, [name redacted]
>   home village, Paldi in the Punjab,
>   builds his pioneer tree-to-log story,
>   Rosedale, near Chilliwack, from Strawberry Hill near New
>   Westminster
start afresh
relocate
royal city to island,
saw you whom my soul loves,
>   *Shri*-श्री [name redacted], acquirer: Island Lumber Co. There is
>   the valley.
Sing it: Cowichan—a song of first peoples, other peoples, pioneer and settler
>   sweater and lumber
>   vegetable and sheep
>   painters and potters
>   Action: Sing! Come to Paldi. Come to Paldi. We will work together. Sing,
>   Canada, all ye nations. In the valley that is Cowichan: Indo-Japanese—live, work.
>   Oh Pioneer Raga. Sing! The man who is *Shri*-श्री [name redacted],
>   will reconfigure time. He will choose a new birthdate. It
>   will be the first of July.

Exhibit: June 4, 1985, in the woods outside Duncan, items of examination

Item A.   Sanyo AM/FM stereo tuner, model number FMT 611K

Interjection: When I was a child—

Item B.   Time.

Interjection: Douglas fir, cedar, clump of alders—splinter sunlight. And

                       shake, the forest floor

Item C.   and after,

Interjection: means nothing

Exhibit: in the woods outside Duncan, June 4, 1985, a woman listens

"Although they were on a surveillance mission, the surveillants did not have a camera"

–Volume One, The Overview, Chapter III, *Commission of [redacted]*

in the woods, outside Duncan
>   a woman sits in a vehicle.
>   [She works for CSIS, also, the RCMP. Where is the name? It is redacted.]

>   Listen—exculpation, ~~attempted~~

>   in-script explode

>   [force   of sound/energy
>   expended
>   enough to rock
>   her up and over]

There is the tunnelling of words
I didn't
think
it was a bomb:
1985,
cross-examined:

Exhibit: "Yes, that's what I said. It didn't sound like a bomb."

     Look, I've taken early retirement. Ask my lawyer.
     Sorry, don't mean to sound rude. It's just—
     haven't we been over this enough times?
     I was doing my job, proud of my work.
     Yes. Yes. How many times have we gone over,

this, sitting and then,
sound—
just rocked me
over—
     I mean the force,
the thing exploded and I fell out
my seat, the whole car jolted.
     Was there any smell? There may have been. I can't recall. Not anymore.

     I was one of the few women hired, you know, it wasn't always easy.
     Of course I took it seriously. Followed him all the way from Vancouver, right?

Exhibit: errata & rogue

un/authorized interjection: *a funeral service will be held at New Life Community Baptist Church, 1839 Tzouhalem Road, Duncan BC followed by cremation, followed by prayers at Paldi Sikh Temple (source: [name redacted])*

*

un/authorized statement: in the after-time, about a man,
            about his explosives:

"on the day of my daughter's wedding, well, he [name redacted], tried to block me from entering the temple. I went in anyway."

            –un/authorized attribution: Shri-श्री [name redacted]

*

un/authorized insistence:
"You know, if they aren't victims,
guess I just think of them
as the bad guys."

            –Informant to N

*

indictment: dear [name redacted]

"against the peace of our Lady the Queen her Crown and Dignity"

Allegation: "This man lied nineteen times."

Equation: man=conviction=name [redacted]=description, "**M**an **I**n **A** **T**urban"= M-I-A-T= Miat.

there, now, a character

*

Nineteen Things about Miat

The voice of god speaks to me. My lips open, close, on the word of scripture.

As a child, I spoke like a child, and ran freely.

There were no signs of the coming years.

June 23, 1985 starts. Stops. Jailed, I live in the light that god and my guru give me.

I will ask those who write about me to assemble a litany of years.

At sixteen, I worked the green chain in a mill. I worked machines.

I am skilled in the making of things—earned my ticket, electrician.

Sound comes at me. Speak. Speak. Do not.

My community is a source of comfort to me. I am not interested in community.

I have no need for the words of any alien tongue.

My outer body is nothing to me. I crave a home-cooked meal.

The woods smelled of cedar and the air was clean.

Deeper and deeper the years, an archive, and I, an entry into 1985 and after—

Each morning, I kiss the words of scripture.

My lawyer understands my story and speaks it.

My children will bear children who will bear children and my family survives.

I did not attend the wedding of my daughter.

Whoever tells my story must add up the years and then discount them.

Minutes and months, days and cycles, these are known to me in the steps of one cell.

I am on good terms with the people who manage my incarceration.

Exhibit: after-time accompaniment, morning raga for Paldi

And there are mountains. And there is water.
And there is that refrain that is for this morning's journey by ferryboat,
   such snippets as will be, will be found
      : saw you whom my soul loves, I say to the watchman
in a Horseshoe Bay coffee shop, the words of—

about the village of Paldi
   outside Duncan
     : saw you whom my soul loves,
    there are the mountains,
and water and words,
there are no expectations of meeting. Meet, the ferry.
    Horseshoe Bay to Nanaimo, up Island, and there is sureness—
   There will be a meeting. There are not facts to suggest it
   Sing(h), this journey, Cowichan Valley.
Now, the ferryboat carries this raga. Now it is sailing.

There are the names, bring them. Insert Punjabi.
There are the places, this is the time, and after—
   June 23, 1985. Insert all dialects and languages
  spoken and dreamt and worked and ploughed and mined and dug and timbered.
There is a body on a ferryboat: Sing(h)!
Queen of Oak Bay to Nanaimo, replication of a journey.
Bomb-maker, poem-maker. Name the name of the man driven to—

Name who boarded a ferryboat! Name the history of the bay,
    and its waters cry, come, *tikka, tikka, otototoi,*
      saw you him who did the deed?
In his path, this replication. And know his end. And know his end.
It is jail. It is obliteration. It is fragments. His ways and means, a bombing.
This is morning-raga-mountains-water.
   This is a sailing to Nanaimo on the *Queen of Oak Bay*—

Exhibit: after-time accompaniment, catechism

What is the echo of grief? A person, layered with history.

What is this name, Paldi? A village called memory.

What is the town, Duncan? Side by side. Separate and apart.

What is this honorific, *Shri-श्री*?

    It is for the man, [name redacted]. It is for his son, [name redacted].

Who are the men and women of the village, of the town? They are there and not there.

What is this intent? Name. Set together. Speak. We never speak of it.

What is this intent? To make a bomb.

What is this intent? To situate a story.

Where is Empire? Here.

What is the name that is the signifier? British/Columbia.

State the time of confession: kneeling before the Guru's scripture, Paldi Sikh Temple.

Who was it, then, to offer *prasad* after prayer? It was the woman, Mrs. [name redacted].

What is the name of any song to be recorded? *Saw you whom my soul loves.*

Exhibit: after-time accompaniment, pilgrimage

How many years? Cannot count them.

How many miles? Speak not of anything but love.

What was the sound? Traffic. A moan-roar of logging trucks on Highway 18.

What are the coordinates? In the woods, off the highway, across from the turnoff,
    Hillcrest Road.

Describe any attributes: Saw no rip-rap. Name the names of the trees.

                              Cannot name the trees.

What was the sound? Pine needles, faded to dust-brown, falling, falling.

        N: "it was pitter-patter. Most benign. A dry rain."

What was the sound? A highway moans.

Describe any attributes: detritus common to those parts:

flayed-open mattress, metal cast-offs, the backside of a digital recorder.

What was the sound? It was the years. It was being there.

List any further observations: not for N, the waters of the Atlantic,

    not for N, candles and puja,

        not Ottawa, not Montreal, not Toronto.

The woods close in.

PART FIVE

and its dimensions

Exhibit: *in camera*

grey-green Atlantic
eighty-two suspensions
                    adrift on the ocean floor—
            transparent as jellyfish—
                    children of Air India
            their long phosphorous arms sway,
sending messages
            undecipherable

This page—a site of research

Somewhere on a tarmac by the ocean, an airplane waits.
It is always waiting
            but we are not on it.
We are not the children of Air India Flight 182.
This is not June 1985.
These words are not under water,
the only oxygen present
is now.

Evening: N's raga

In the hour past sundown
kitchen counter query:
        what is it to prepare a meal, to eat it alone? This is the work of grief.
            Memory-muscle, used, re-used
              time before 1985
                  at supper's table, a father prays
                 —bless this food to our use—
                    in whose name did he speak, voice dry
as if the winds of south central Saskatchewan had over the years borne him
              not one Chinook, only short rustlings
              inside his chest
           Gather round, four-person family, here is 1985
                spiralling always to time's centre
      the puff of a belly, the meat of a child's arm—
lucky evening that takes its purpose from light
and fades.

Outside, bats glide, quick now, the after-time,
intent on shadow, shadows of—
           image-Atlantic imagining number
           eighty-two under the age thirteen
outside N walks to see the bats, soundless,
their fine teeth hidden. Outside, time's wheel
           turning
           ocean, conjured, reflected on concrete
here, now, the street,
           in boulevard's grasses, recollection as amulet
           other people's stories,
         three hundred and thirty one bodies
digest the night deepening to moon, illuminated evanescence.

Testimony: her name was [redacted]

She was seven years old.
Her mother said: she was full of life.
Her mother said: she was very pretty.
Her mother said: she loved to dance.
Her mother said: she loved music.
Her name was [redacted].
She was seven years old.

Exhibit (1985): the unknown family

We are mother-father-daughter-daughter:
>   three of us India-born, one of us Canada-made,
> each grain of each minute, cascading days:
the 1960s rush into the 1970s rush into a new decade
1980—
no signs come to us
>   that we might one day end, no portents accumulate
>   to brush against our skin
>   time marks out year one to year five in the new decade,
>   no wash of recognition,
that this forward movement will
end-stop.
>   The rub of our lives
>   goes on and that morning—

>   my husband rolls his shoulders
>   to me, his chest, my chin, in the heat we've created
>   darkness to daylight his brown skin smooth my brown skin
>   smooth arm, leg, in movement soon
>   sweat, gossamer fine covers us
>   in me a five-lettered opening—
>   Shiva   Radha
>   two others I will not name
>   (fragments intrude into sleep, all these years
>   alone, alone
>   husband entering,
>   in our marriage bed there is room for his sex, and mine
>   flowers
>   each fold a skin-push,
>   tissue of our flesh, sweet-bitter
>   in that way morning one on one, two together
>   arranged and of volition
>   but *Shush,* and *Now, now, now—*
>   *We don't want to wake the girls*

my husband's fingertips—
nipple's edge, outlined,
one breast, in one hand,
our girls pretending sleep, early so early in that hour just
before dawn,
the day before—

Status: bodies unfound

Exhibit (1985): son

Mississauga mornings
life surrounds me:
mother, her almond eyes,
on me each lap I swim, Mother
her fine, pinched nose inhales
the scent of me, chlorine lad swimming
her plans   boundless
surrounding me, each lap success:

       be a doctor, behave,
           be fast, these community recreation waters
lane to lane, head(s) up! Mother—
       I down-rhythm away from her
in water all admonishments chased
butterfly,
       breaststroke
       stoking time,
       boarding the plane,
       taking me into
       this other—

Exhibit (1985): so proud

Achievement, a ship—
                and I sailed her,
      first class: music, math biology
94.5 per cent average,
          University of Toronto
          full medical scholarship.
These are the accolades set down for me—
My parents. And love.

un/authorized coda:
Although there is no record, let the record show:
          saxophone, drums, trumpet and flute
brass, silver, skin and wood
wind
held my secrets

          fled with my body, unheard melody
I have kept my own dissonance,
          beyond the reach of school grades and exams

no expectations of excellence rose as a shield
          against explosion.

I am my own test,
          disintegrated,
          unfound.

Exhibit (1985): Trois Rivières

(if there is English it is for E—

Action:

        three young women make friends with Québéecois girls—
           learn French,
       play games in the snow

Longing: home: Quebec, India
Border: French, English, Punjabi

Mother:

        on an icy side street, snow packed high and heavy, wet—
          a woman in a saree and short boots,
           negotiates her path, one foot before another,
             slow—
          heel raised, then down,
             one hand as if to reach for something
             what? the air?
       She grasps at silk, action as juncture
          where winter ends   her fabric,
      begins—

Sister: Look, look at me— I'm a snow angel   my arms, wings!

Status: mother and sister, deceased.

Mother and Daughter,

Your body always under mother's eye travelling companion she sees
Your breasts rise fall tight shirt pulsating sixteen impenetrable under mother's eye
Your smooth black hair flowing s-shaped crown oiled night in the bathroom
  upstairs
Your kingdom North American suburban home always there is the mother-natter
Your grades your clothes you're not wearing that on the plane cover yourself
Your big flight dress up it is an event. Your tightest jeans. Your mother scolds.
Your obedience wearing chiffon and it is dressy folds *remember to iron your slip*
Your two-inch strappy sandals in the airport mother's eye up down
Your washroom stall manoeuvre nylons peel off hand to feet this is flesh its release
Your eyes never to be mother never to suckle a child. Also there is aunt. Also,
        there is grandmother these links generations waiting to board on the plane
        it is hours
You talk grades talk school talk story within story your aunt-mother-grandmother
    your family—tale of tales within languagefablegossipsecretsanecdotal
    listening not listening
Your mother's words dense sticky gumming your gloss coated lips trailing conversation
Your mother's love smothering love and envy love and watching love jealousy love
    eyeing
Up and down love interrogation love assessment love getting love amassing love grimy
Your love lies gritty on your tongue: the conversation of four women. You will talk. You
will sigh. You will go to the toilet, twice, three times,
        cramped, the light inside the stall green-tinged,
        acrid whiff of smoke
            the hours—
    them. You,
    on Air India Flight 182.
    You are sixteen,
    soon to be released, scattered. Soon.
You are with your women-mouth-teeth-tongue-lips curl lift open sound laughter
    Speak, Punjabi! There is the sometimes-in-English-all-women-story talk:
    It is all weaving family-fabric, not unlike the chiffon of your dress, light but it sticks
Your full breasts. Your ears hearing not hearing the words
Your own words said to yourself they will never get to hear about a boy in Chem 11

About his fair hair his arms that will hold his watching you his mouth it might move
against
You your thighs in the airplane seat you clench-release,
    buttocks, legs, feet, hands,
        fingers
            knuckles not swollen, not bruised, young and clench,
   release, this summer trip—your body, your family multiple of four
It is the mother-line stretching–soon it will be broken—soon all the words
   you will have said you will not say disintegrate and drop
        dropping
      thirty thousand feet,
      air dense,
      air made
      steel,

        sharp impact against breasts   hips,
     your groin pulsing   pulse and, and—

Balcony Song: N's redactions

In the rain your names come to me
        Dr.—(Aunty!)
        Dr.—(Uncle!)
        family taken out of time
        fractured, still strong
        in the morning
where airborne
solace descends
rain-fed—
            grass on the surface of land far below,
                  the view drops, the river, south-side
            after two months of no rain, patchy barren yellow yearning
for green to come by rain, aunt's smile, dew-diamond in her nose
            flash the rain-soaked days: what year is it?
in the after-time, time
        reflects
fronds of a geranium, green scented
        a petal glows scarlet-fragrance
this coloured
candescent air, ~~alive~~.   Alive.

Exhibit: mother of the after-time

On Air India Flight 182, a husband and a daughter board the plane.
They are their own unit.

Left behind, the son.
Left behind, the mother.

*

Daughter: I am seven. Stroke my cheeks! They are and were. They are and were.
Mother: It is rose petals.
Daughter: Where are my hands?
Mother: turning and turning—
Daughter: Where are my feet?
Mother: Lifting, lifted
Daughter: Why did you come?
Mother: There is your father. There is India. I will stay back. I will work.
Mother and Daughter: we will be together.

*

June 23, 1985, early the phone rings. After, she does not cry.
Not that week, taut nights full of business.

After, night and day, she is the mother. They will return.

After, she is the mother and there is the waiting;
    so much business is expectation, is phone calls, is messages from strangers,

Notes from the coroner: "We found them. A miracle. They are alive!"

None of these things happen.

After, she does not cry, after elongates and looks at her: full-of-business single
    mother, there is the son. He does not board the plane.

After, the years are loss and that is her work. Look at her. She travels the country,
    memorials' emissary. She lays wreaths. The years rush by. No daughter:

no graduation, no wedding plans.
The register neither confirms nor denies the finding of a body.
How smooth the skin of this mother, delicate as rose petals. She wears a saree.

In the after-time it is twenty-five and after, the years.
Mother: Where is my son?
News: There is airplane. There is attack.
Son: This is the after-time and I am in it.
Mother: Remember.

After there is sound—
more sustained than a clock ticking, or a computer click-whirring,

fridge humming there is sound louder than
any electronic device anywhere beep-chirping   shush, shush—

There is sound: here is the after-room where the after-mother sits
Name the sound. ~~Name the mother~~. She is the after-

mother. **Daughter:** Speak not of anything but love
Mother: These tears are after—

You may think these statements are hypothetical about unreal people.
There is the after-mother. She is always with her memorials.

There is the daughter. There is the weight. It is Atlantic.
There is the water. It is a morning raga. After and after.

Oh my father's servants, bring my palanquin.
I am going to the land of my husband.

Imagine, then, the families of the children of Air India

Exhibit: here in Stanley Park

      and left behind
           a son, [name redacted]

He is alabaster
He is in the gloaming, his sandals   evening over   stones
rock   dirt   a newly rolled lawn
      it is the after-time

      Ireland   India
          Ireland   Canada
      Atlantic   Pacific
          Columbia, that is British and ~~Quebec~~ that is
          we never speak of it
      and left behind, also

  Informant to N, voice rising: "It wasn't
          just brown people, you know"

1985 and after in the after-time a son wanders here are fragments as relations.
If there is a Lord, he is as remnant-informant to N, holding newspaper: "I read
  about him"

    a son walks alongside a stone wall
          long fingers tapering to stone. There is a mother—

        her name on a wall, and behind the wall,
      ocean,
        and behind waters   light
      fades
        behind a horizon—

All these connections.
Detonation's family.

N's evening raga

: rise and go,

        search the world for its one true Book of Records,
        find the names of children
            entered, set down beyond longing—
   all the children, everywhere, in every epoch and age,
   cut, scooped out, broken and scattered, buried in soil and water,
          children under the age of thirteen—
               every nation, field and river with its own register
               clenching at names
                   written in ink implacably invisible
                       only the cool-fire resident
                       in the tips of fingers that trace
                       in the hands of a beloved leaning
                       into a lectern, oak or marble,
                       raised on a dais, this transmission
                          great gilt-edged thing
          only the ice-fire of the loved ones of these
                     dead children, will burn alive
                     will make legible
                     their inscription

Exhibit: Z, 1943–1985

—why haven't you set down the exact date of her birth?

—Sister! Muslims do not celebrate birthdays. Speak to us, speak to us.

N (eyes downcast): Forgive.

—this evidence: unreliable. These witnesses, unmitigated   in fact,

—uncertainties abound, the whiteness of this page a fog of memory—any
    information I share is subject to whatever mistakes you will make—she was
    my youngest sister—

N (eyes downcast): forgive

—heinous crime, preponderance of fact, unreasonable. And there is doubt

N (eyes downcast): all water washes me

—Your mother asked so I am sending

—in my courtroom there is no room for error—

N (eyes downcast): youngest in the family, she secured very high marks. Medical
    college. M.B., B.Sc., D.G.O., M.D. (gynaecology and obstetrics) and—

un/authorized interjection: tell us, why won't you, her seat number on the plane

N (eyes downcast): officer in the National Cadet Corps, reserve army for
    university students Welcomed (our) Queen in New Delhi,

—against the peace of our Lady the Queen her Crown and Dignity, speak not of
    any indictments, I banished [name redacted], exonerated [name redacted]
    and,

N (eyes downcast): contingent. Also, was part of a group that climbed a mountain in the Himalayas and,

—not Everest, but some other about half Everest's height, I'm guessing here. Why didn't you incorporate my words, earlier? I wrote you ten years ago!

N (eyes downcast): forgive

Ghost Sutra

another sentencing hearing begins in Vancouver on Wednesday for [name redacted]

to me, my countryman—of what you did and never will do,

from the island town of Duncan, province where we live,

there are the songs of Canada/India,

of what we are, what we've become—

the only man ever convicted in connection with the Air India bombing

Sing to me children, of what you were, and now: restless and travelling—

We will never hear [him] say the truth

my countryman   minutes and hours, jailed with you—

Some family members of those killed in the Air India bombing planned to be in the
courtroom—

aunt, uncle, sing
of what you were and will be,
1985 and after—

Water, wind
child and limb,
bomb and island   Air India, rock, where cuts the rain

no ocean like time, no ocean like time

For an Afterword That Might Be Read as a Preface

"If ever there was a woman whose life is the very symbol of cultural diversity...
born in India, she arrived in Canada with her parents as an infant. Her mother was
Muslim, her father a Hindu who converted to Christianity and became a United
Church minister. She's lived in Newfoundland, Quebec, Saskatchewan and British
Columbia."

–Jim Brown, Canadian Press, 2006

October 5, 2006: note

    : on a raised dais under the gaze of Mr. Justice Major.

: about what it feels like: to be related to the dead of Air India—

    out of range of forward-vision,

the writer, Jim Brown, from the Canadian Press.

*

Days later: *and his words stay with me*

*

A central experience of being held within the saga that is Air India is one of
forgetting/remembering. The events leading up to the bombing, the act itself
and its aftermath, are well documented, are obscured within the mainstream of
Canadian culture. As the niece of family members who died in the bombing, this
impulse—remember, forget—propels memorial and its counter-forms, seeing in
those things and processes, in dense, layered story, time and its materials. Imagine,
then, that which becomes enacted each year, at the end of June, the anniversary of
the bombing of an airplane. But these notions come to me only slowly, in the act
of creating individual pieces, and then looking back, fed by everything else, all the

detritus, the flotsam and jetsam, the archive that is Air India Flight 182, which is its own current that is the entity, Canada: reports, news stories, legal proceedings, volumes amassed, set aside. Add also the relatively new genre of scholarly research into the events of June 23, 1985 and after, and there develops an ecosphere, a habitat that surrounds any public/private tragedy—an environment containing the remains of violent acts, cultural artifacts, personal stories, investigation, as well as exhaustion and longing. And underneath, everlastingly, the loss of 329 people plus 2 more.

*

Recollection: that day

there are people in the Bytown Pavilion on Sussex Drive, Ottawa, the nation's capital, and most of us cluster in Victoria Hall. A lawyer, Howard Mickelson, counsel for the families of the Air India dead, Western Canada—
(yes, the Commission categorizes us by way of that old shibboleth of our nation: west, divided from east)—Howard reminds me of the provinces across Canada where I have lived.   .
that day : speaking about what it feels like to be Canadian, to be part of this
     particular saga,

                              that day

: seeing and not : a man who sits in the rows before the Commissioner. He is
     writing—

*

Write the names all the way through. Write them down.

In writing there is redaction, redact.

That is the burning that is the body.

Sources Consulted

The Families Remember, Commission of Inquiry into the Investigation of the Bombing of Air India Flight 182, John C. Major, Commissioner.

A Reader's Guide, Air India Flight 182: A Canadian Tragedy, Commission of Inquiry.

Air India Inquiry Opening Statement, June 21, 2006, the Honourable John C. Major on the release of the report of the Commission of Inquiry.

Air India Flight 182: A Canadian Tragedy: Commission of Inquiry Final Report, Volume One, The Overview; Volume Two, Part 1: Pre-Bombing.

Witness statements: October 5, 2006, Commission of Inquiry/Air India: Public Hearings, Bytown Pavilion, Ottawa.

Site visits: September 19, 2011: in the woods, off Highway 18, at Hillcrest Road, outside Duncan, British Columbia; Paldi Sikh Temple; home of Joan Cameron Mayo, Paldi/Duncan, British Columbia.

Site visits: numerous occasions, Stanley Park, Vancouver, British Columbia.

Zhindagee: Voices of Canadian Asian Indian First Daughters 1920–1950, Mahinder Kaur Doman Manhas, Editor, 2010 (7/1000 original copies).

Paldi Remembered: Fifty Years in the Life of a Vancouver Island Logging Town, Joan Cameron Mayo

BCGNIS Geographical Name Query Results.

"Representations of Murdered and Missing Women," *west coast line 53* (2007), Anne Stone and Amber Dean, editors.

"Remembering the Air India Disaster: Memorial and Counter-Memorial," Angela Failler, *Review of Education, Pedagogy, and Cultural Studies*, 31: 150–176 (2009).

Participation: Memorial: "Canada Remembers," in commemoration of the twenty-fifth anniversary of the Air India Flight 182 Tragedy, Stanley Park, Vancouver, June, 2010.

Air India Trial, Media Information Package, Regina v Ripudaman Singh Malik and Ajaib Singh Bagri, April 2003.

Courtroom 20: Vancouver Law Courts, Ministry of Attorney General, Government of British Columbia.

"What Was Behind Me Now Faces Me: Performance, staging and technology in the court of law," Judy Radul, *Glanta/ Eurozine*, 2007.

"The Medico-legal Organization of a Mass Disaster: The Air India crash 1985," CT
    Doyle, MA Bolster, Dept of Pathology, Cork Regional Hospital, Cork, Ireland.

*

Sample of newspaper clippings consulted, 1985–2011

From a manila envelope, carried around for years:

Vancouver Sun: Thursday, June 22, 2000; Wednesday, September 12, 2001;
    February–May 2003.

Province, Sunday, November 12, 2002.

Vancouver Sun, Thursday, February 13, 2003.

Globe and Mail, Tuesday February 11, 2003.

National Post, Thursday, February 13, 2003.

Globe and Mail, Thursday, October 5, 2006.

*

**From a blue and white folder, embossed with the imprimatur of the
Commission of Inquiry into the Investigation of the Bombing of Air India
Flight 182:**

Printed online story from canada.com, Canadian Press, Jim Brown Thursday,
    October 5, 2006, "Air India families tell of shock, disillusion in aftermath of
    bombing."

Promotional Flyer for the World Television Premiere, CBC Television, June 22,
    2008 at 9 p.m., "Air India 182," Sturla Gunnarsson, director.

"Rules of Procedure and Practice," Commission of Inquiry.

Multiple drafts, speaking notes, R. Saklikar, and statement, B. Saklikar, October,
    2006, Victoria Hall, Bytown Pavilion, 111 Sussex Drive, Ottawa, Ontario.

Terms of Reference, Commission of Inquiry, Privy Council-Conseil Privé, "Her
    Excellency the Governor General in Council, on the recommendation of the
    Prime Minister, hereby directs that a Commission do issue…"(P.C. 2006–293,
    May 1).

"City of New Westminster to apologize to Chinese Canadians for past injustices,"
    Charlie Smith, *The Georgia Straight*, June 30, 2010.

"Still Lingers On: The Sixtieth Anniversary of the Internment. Part I, "No Alternative," Tom. I Tagami, Nikkei Images, *Japanese Canadian National Museum Newsletter*, Spring, 2002, Vol. 7, No.1.

"Welcome to Paldi, BC Canada"—online/internet source, link unknown.

Obituary Notice, Sands of Duncan, MAYO, Rajindi Singh, Paldi, BC 1933–2008.

*

Loss of Faith: How the Air-India Bombers Got Away with Murder, Kim Bolan (McClelland & Stewart, 2005).

Margin of Terror, Salim Jiwa and Donald Hauka (Jaico, 2008).

The Sorrow and the Terror, Clark Blaise and Bharati Mukherjee (Viking, 1987).

Email correspondence with Clark Blaise, July 2008.

Conversations with Hari Sharma, summer 2008.

Email correspondence with Alan Twigg, July 23, 2010.

Conversations with Kim Bolan, 1985–ongoing.

Conversations with Charlie Smith, Editor, *The Georgia Straight*, ongoing.

Conversations with Gurpreet Singh, 2010; conversations with Naveen Girn, ongoing.

Family conversation and correspondence.

*

"Coping with Racism: One Minister's Story," Vasant Saklikar, *Mandate, Canada's Cultural Mosaic,* (United Church of Canada) 1989.

1984 Sikhs' Kristallnacht, Parvinder Singh, Gurdwara Sahib Dasmesh Darbar.

"Refracting Pacific Canada, Seeing our Uncommon Past," Henry Yu, *BC Studies,* No. 156/157, Winter/Spring, 2007/08.

"Do we apologize to the victims of the Air India Bombing?" [name redacted], C--W News, radio online email circular, June 18, 2010.

"Bloody Sunday: How the Truth Came Out," Harold Evans, blog essay, *The Daily Beast,* June 16, 2010.

Acknowledgements

Conversations with Wayde Compton about *Diamond Grill* (NeWest, 1996) by Fred Wah.

Conversations with Rachel Rose about *Holocaust* (Black Sparrow, 1975) and *Testimony* (Black Sparrow, 1965) by Charles Reznikoff.

Conversation with Rolf Maurer about this work and about Lisa Robertson's *Debbie: An Epic* (New Star, 1997) and *The Weather* (New Star, 2001).

Conversations with Sandy Shreve about the Air India story and iterations of this work.

Conversations with Don McKay at Piper's Frith 2011, Kilmory, Newfoundland.

Attendance at a performance of *Zong!* by M. NourbeSe Philip, and in conversation with the author, November 29, 2009, Vancouver.

Conversation with Jen Currin about Tim O Brien's *The Things They Carried* (Houghton Mifflin, 1990).

Attendance at a presentation by Michael Turner, "to show, to give, to make it be there: Expanded Literary Practices in Vancouver: 1954–1969," Simon Fraser University, and in conversations with him, and found shortly thereafter in a second-hand antiques store down on Front Street, by the Fraser River, New Westminster, BC: "Journal of a Voyage," Malcom Lowry, *The Paris Review 23*.

Conversations with Betsy Warland and with Ray Hsu, on the nature of transgression.

Performance and Collaboration, English to Punjabi, "Flying Across Canada to Ireland," Indo-Canadian Workers Association, June 2011—Mohan Gill and Renée Saklikar.

Conversations with J. Janzen about this manuscript (earlier iteration), summer 2011.

Conversations with D.Harder about *The Girl in Saskatoon: A Meditation of Friendship, Memory and Murder*, Sharon Butala and *New Moon at Batoche, Reflections on the Urban Prairie*, George Melnyk and then a reading of both those works, summer 2010.

Witness/poem performance, December 6, 2009, in the alley behind the Vancouver Police Station, off Cordova Street, Vancouver, memorial for Frank Joseph Paul.

Held in a cover of deerskin, beaded border, embroidered with the sign of the cross: *The Holy Bible*, King James Version, World Publishing Company, Cleveland, Ohio.

"at the origin of error there will always be a 'slip'... not by the subject, but by... his (sic) written or oral 'informant'" *Oral Tragedy*, Dorothy Lusk (chapbook, Tsunami Editions, Lary Bremner, editor).

An early version of this manuscript, "Part One," appeared in *Ryga: a journal of provocations*, Number 5, 2012—with thanks to Sean Johnston.

Translations:

Punjabi: Balkaran Singh ("The Censor That Is Time")

Irish Gaelic: Caitríona Ní Chonchúir ("The Censor That Is Time")

French: Elodie Jacquet (Coroner's Report)

*

Thanks to Silas White, Carleton Wilson, Lizette Fischer and everyone at Nightwood Editions.

*

for my husband, without whom
for my father, absent/still present
for my mother and for my sister, ~~we never speak of it~~
for Irfan—

a blewointment book

In 1963, bill bissett founded blewointmentpress in Vancouver and began publishing mimeographed magazines of experimental poetry. Within a few years bissett, known for his own work in sound and concrete poetry, began to publish books that subversively extended the boundaries of language, visual image and political statement, including work by bpNichol, Steve McCaffery, Andrew Suknaski, Lionel Kearns, Maxine Gadd, d.a. levy & bissett himself. Meeting wide acclaim and controversy, the activities of blewointmentpress have had a seminal influence on the Canadian literary community.

After a drastic reduction in government support in 1982, the press stuggled with debt and bissett sold blewointment. It was renamed Nightwood Editions by Maureen Cochrane & David Lee. After a couple more incarnations of the press moving bissett-like back and forth across the country and publishing work as diverse as poetry, fiction, film & music criticism and children's titles, Nightwood launched a "blewointment" imprint in 2005 to honour bissett and the press's innovative, political and visual roots.

BLEWOINTMENT TITLES AVAILABLE FROM NIGHTWOOD EDITIONS:

False Maps for Other Creatures by Jay MillAr, poetry: 978-0-88971-203-4 (2005)

radiant danse uv being: a poetic portrait of bill bissett edited by Jeff Pew & Stephen Roxborough, anthology: 978-0-88971-210-2 (2006)

Hitch by Matthew Holmes, poetry: 978-0-88971-214-0 (2006)

Birch Split Bark by Diane Guichon, poetry 978-0-88971-215-7 (2007)

forage by Rita Wong, poetry: 978-0-88971-213-3 (2007)

Other Poems by Jay MillAr, poetry: 978-0-88971-242-3 (2010)

Err by Shane Rhodes, poetry: 978-0-88971-256-0 (2011)

Undark by Sandy Pool, poetry: 978-0-88971-273-7 (2012)

X by Shane Rhodes, poetry: 978-0-88971-288-1 (2013)

Timely Irreverence by Jay MillAr, poetry: 978-0-88971-277-5 (2013)

Children of Air India by Renée Sarojini Saklikar, poetry: 978-0-88971-287-4 (2013)

For more information on these titles please browse: www.nightwoodeditions.com

About the Author

Renée Sarojini Saklikar writes thecanadaproject, a lifelong poem chronicle about her life from India to Canada, from coast to coast. Work from thecanadaproject appears in literary publications including *The Georgia Straight*, *The Vancouver Review*, *PRISM international*, *Poetry is Dead*, *SubTerrain*, *Ricepaper*, *CV2*, *Ryga: a journal of provocations*, *Geist* and *Arc Poetry Magazine* and in the recent anthologies, *Alive at the Center:Contemporary Poems from the Pacific Northwest* and *Force Field: 77 Women Poets of British Columbia*. *Children of Air India* is her debut collection.

thecanadaproject.wordpress.com

PHOTO CREDIT: Ayelet Tsabari

Photo Your Mother, Your Aunt and Uncle, You at the Vancouver Airport 1985

Your Mother wears an Indian outfit/ you and she stand on one side of a glass barrier
a wall/ separation /between/ going staying
Your mother's hand rests on a wooden ledge/dark coloured/
a horizontal line running the length of the photograph
Your Mother a bookend/ one side of the scene
and you/ the other
You wear a blue cotton top/ white cotton pants
On the other side of the glass/ light/ tarmac behind them your aunt and uncle
in a corridor framed by two sides of glass
Your aunt/separated/glass/barrier/you
Your mother uncle/to one side/behind her
Mother, Aunt, Uncle, You
Who frames the photograph/takes the picture/adjusts the camera
Camera Vancouver Airport Leaving/ coming and going
Tickets tickets/ your father Unnamed/ Absent
Who is behind your father standing with his hand
behind me out-of-sight/ absent/ faces/ poses/ photograph/still/
framed moment/motion/

VOLUME ONE
THE OVERVIEW

CHAPTER II: THE INQUIRY PROCESS

MR. ████████: ...] There's been some reference in our hearings to a culture of secrecy that pervades Ottawa. Do you have any comment on that characterization?

MR. ████████: I think it's an accurate characterization.

MR. ████████: Accurate or inaccurate?

MR. ████████: Accurate. It's accurate. We over classify, we over-redact and then we ultimately get embarrassed by it being shown to not have been necessary so many times. I think it's just in the nature of the beast, and that happens all the time, and it happens continuously before every inquiry that seems to take place. We start from the position of we're not going to share, we're not going to show anything because we don't want to reveal anything and then, ultimately, we have to reveal, and we have to show, and the system gets embarrassed because of some redacts, you know, classifications that were clearly inappropriate and so on.